Presented to

_____

by_____

on _____

What about Heaven?

Kathleen Long Bostrom
Illustrated by Elena Kucharik

TYNDALE
KIDS

Tyndale House Publishers, Inc.
WHEATON, ILLINOIS

Library of Congress Cataloging-in-Publication Data

Bostrom, Kathleen Long.
   What about heaven? / Kathleen Long Bostrom.
      p. cm — (Questions from little hearts)
      Summary: A rhyming text consisting of a child's questions about heaven, the responses
given, and scriptural references to support the answers.
      ISBN 0-8423-7353-5 (hc : alk. paper)
      1. Heaven—Christianity—Miscellanea—Juvenile literature. 2. Heaven—Quotations,
maxims, etc.—Juvenile literature. 3. Bible—Quotations—Juvenile literature. [1. Heaven.2.
Bible—Selections.] I. Title. II. Series.
BT849 .B67 2000
236'.24—dc21   99-053852

Printed in Italy

09 08 07 06 05 04 03 02
10 9 8 7 6 5

*To my sister, Rebecca, and my brother, John,
with unending love.*

*Thank you to the following people at Tyndale House
for their grace and kindness:
Betty, Carla, Cathy, Karen, and Travis.
And thank you to Elena Kucharik, whose wonderful
Little Blessings characters bring these books to life.*

I know that God loves me.

Of this there's no doubt.

But what about heaven?

What's that all about?

Is heaven a place

that is near or that's far?

Can I get to heaven

by boat or by car?

How will I find it?

Who'll show me the way?

6

Does heaven have nighttime?

And what about day?

8

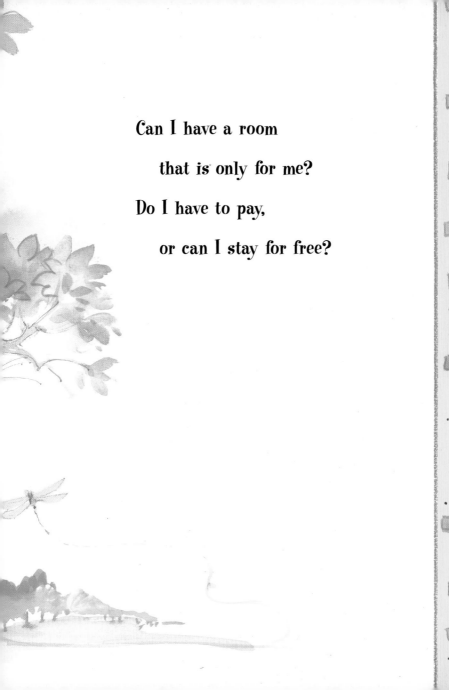

Can I have a room

that is only for me?

Do I have to pay,

or can I stay for free?

Will I look the very

same way I do now?

Will everyone know

who I am? If so, how?

What food will I eat?

And what clothes will I wear?

When I get to heaven,

who else will be there?

Does heaven have mountains,

and trees I can climb?

What will I do there

with all of my time?

Is there enough space

for the animals, too?

Will there be some kind

of a heavenly zoo?

Since God is in heaven,

it has to be great.

Can I go there now,

or do I have to wait?

All questions have answers,

but some you won't learn

Till God says it's time

for his Son to return.

Your questions are good ones,

so let's dive right in

And see what the Bible says.

Ready? Begin!

Though heaven's a place

that you can't see from here,

It says in the Bible

that heaven is near.

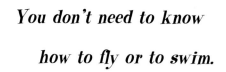

You don't need to know

how to fly or to swim.

The way is with Jesus,

believing in him.

It always is daytime–

there never is night.

The light of God's love

will be shining so bright.

Jesus will give you

a room of your own,

With others nearby

so you won't feel alone.

27

Your body will change

so it's perfect and new,

And yet you will still be

the very same you.

But here's something different,

and this is no trick:

In heaven nobody

will ever get sick!

Our hurts will be healed,

and the deaf will all hear.

The blind will see clearly.

There's nothing to fear!

Everyone there

will be able to talk,

To sing and to dance,

and to run and to walk.

In heaven God serves you

the very best meal.

You'll never be hungry–

now that's a good deal!

The clothes that you'll wear

will be white and so clean;

In heaven you won't need

a washing machine!

Even the animals

won't want to fight;

They'll all get along—

they will not scratch or bite.

Though time has no ending,

    you'll never get bored;

For thousands of years

    seem like days to the Lord.

Heaven is full

of such beautiful things:

The music of millions of

angels who sing.

Rivers like crystal

and seas smooth as glass,

Emeralds glowing

like green springtime grass.

Mountains and jewels

of every type,

Trees full of fruits

that are juicy and ripe.

Sadness and pain

will be taken away;

Once you are there,

you'll be happy to stay.

All of God's children,

the young and the old,

Will gather together

on streets made of gold.

And then there will be

such a grand celebration

When heaven and earth

have become one creation!

Life will be perfect,

for heaven's the place

We'll see God, the Father

and Son, face-to-face.

For God will be there,

everywhere that you are;

And Jesus will shine

like a bright morning star.

Heaven is wonderful,
don't you agree?
It's simply the best place
we ever could be!

Bible References

Here are some Bible verses to talk about as you read this book again with your child. You may want to open your Bible as you read the verses. This will help your little one understand that Jesus' answers in this poem come from his Word, the Bible.

I'm Jesus, God's Son, and I want you to see
The Bible can teach you a lot about me.
I came from my Father to show you the way
To live as God wants you to live every day.

All questions have answers, but some you won't learn
Till God says it's time for his Son to return.
Your questions are good ones, so let's dive right in
And see what the Bible says. Ready? Begin!

Everything that is now hidden or secret will eventually be brought to light. MARK 4:22

All that I know now is partial and incomplete, but then I will know everything completely, just as God knows me now. 1 CORINTHIANS 13:12

**Though heaven's a place that you can't see from here,
It says in the Bible that heaven is near.**

Turn from your sins and turn to God, because the Kingdom of Heaven is near. MATTHEW 3:2

**You don't need to know how to fly or to swim.
The way is with Jesus, believing in him.**

For God so loved the world that he gave his only Son, so that everyone who believes in him will not perish but have eternal life. JOHN 3:16

I am the resurrection and the life. Those who believe in me, even though they die like everyone else, will live again. They are given eternal life for believing in me and will never perish. JOHN 11:25-26

When everything is ready, I will come and get you, so that you will always be with me where I am. JOHN 14:3

It always is daytime–there never is night.
The light of God's love will be shining so bright.

Its gates never close at the end of day because there is
no night. REVELATION 21:25

There will be no night there—no need for lamps or sun—
for the Lord God will shine on them. REVELATION 22:5

Jesus will give you a room of your own
With others nearby so you won't feel alone.

There are many rooms in my Father's home, and I am
going to prepare a place for you. JOHN 14:2

**Your body will change so it's perfect and new,
And yet you will still be the very same you.**

We, too, wait anxiously for that day when God will give us our full rights as his children, including the new bodies he has promised us. ROMANS 8:23

There are bodies in the heavens, and there are bodies on earth. The glory of the heavenly bodies is different from the beauty of the earthly bodies.
1 CORINTHIANS 15:40

We grow weary in our present bodies, and we long for the day when we will put on our heavenly bodies like new clothing. For we will not be spirits without bodies, but we will put on new heavenly bodies.
2 CORINTHIANS 5:2-3

**But here's something different, and this is no trick:
In heaven nobody will ever get sick!**

> Our earthly bodies . . . will be different when they are
> resurrected, for they will never die. They are natural
> human bodies now, but when they are raised, they will
> be spiritual bodies. I CORINTHIANS 15:42, 44

**Our hurts will be healed, and the deaf will all hear.
The blind will see clearly. There's nothing to fear!**

> In that day deaf people will hear words read from a
> book, and blind people will see through the gloom and
> darkness. ISAIAH 29:18

> Our perishable earthly bodies must be transformed into
> heavenly bodies that will never die. I CORINTHIANS 15:53

> The troubles we see will soon
> be over. 2 CORINTHIANS 4:18

**Everyone there will be able to talk,
To sing and to dance, and to run and to walk.**

The people of God will sing a song of joy. ISAIAH 30:29

Those who wait on the Lord will find new strength. They will fly high on wings like eagles. They will run and not grow weary. They will walk and not faint. ISAIAH 40:31

**In heaven God serves you the very best meal.
You'll never be hungry—now that's a good deal!**

The Lord Almighty will spread a wonderful feast for everyone around the world. It will be a delicious feast of good food. ISAIAH 25:6

I will come in, and we will share a meal as friends. REVELATION 3:20

They will never again be hungry or thirsty. REVELATION 7:16

The clothes that you'll wear will be white and so clean;
In heaven you won't need a washing machine!

All who are victorious will be clothed in white.
REVELATION 3:5

They were clothed in white and held palm branches
in their hands. REVELATION 7:9

Even the animals won't want to fight;
They'll all get along—they will not scratch or bite.

In that day the wolf and the lamb will live together;
the leopard and the goat will be at peace. Calves and
yearlings will be safe among lions. . . . The cattle will graze
among bears. Cubs and calves will lie down together.
And lions will eat grass as the livestock do. ISAIAH 11:6-7

Though time has no ending, you'll never get bored;
For thousands of years seem like days to the Lord.

For you, a thousand years are as yesterday! They are like
a few hours! PSALM 90:4

A day is like a thousand years to the Lord, and a
thousand years is like a day. 2 PETER 3:8

Heaven is full of such beautiful things: The music of millions of angels who sing.

Then I looked again, and I heard the singing of thousands and millions of angels around the throne and the living beings and the elders. REVELATION 5:11

Rivers like crystal and seas smooth as glass, Emeralds glowing like green springtime grass.

The glow of an emerald circled his throne like a rainbow. REVELATION 4:3

In front of the throne was a shiny sea of glass. REVELATION 4:6

The angel showed me a pure river with the water of life, clear as crystal. REVELATION 22:1

Mountains and jewels of every type, Trees full of fruits that are juicy and ripe.

Nothing will hurt or destroy in all my holy mountain. ISAIAH 11:9

He took me in spirit to a great, high mountain.
REVELATION 21:10

The wall of the city was built on foundation stones
inlaid with twelve gems: the first was jasper, the second
sapphire, the third agate, the fourth emerald, the fifth
onyx, the sixth carnelian, the seventh chrysolite, the
eighth beryl, the ninth topaz, the tenth chrysoprase,
the eleventh jacinth, the twelfth amethyst.
REVELATION 21:19-20

On each side of the river grew a tree of life, bearing
twelve crops of fruit, with a fresh crop each month.
REVELATION 22:2

Sadness and pain will be taken away;
Once you are there, you'll be happy to stay.

The Sovereign Lord will wipe away all tears. ISAIAH 25:8

Sorrow and mourning will disappear, and they will be
overcome with joy and gladness. ISAIAH 51:11

He will remove all of their sorrows, and there will be
no more death or sorrow or crying or pain.
REVELATION 21:4

All of God's children, the young and the old,
Will gather together on streets made of gold.

All who are victorious will inherit all these blessings,
and I will be their God, and they will be my children.
REVELATION 21:7

The main street was pure gold,
as clear as glass.
REVELATION 21:21

**And then there will be such a grand celebration
When heaven and earth have become one creation!**

All creation anticipates the day when it will join God's children in glorious freedom from death and decay. ROMANS 8:21

Then I saw a new heaven and a new earth, for the old heaven and the old earth had disappeared. REVELATION 21:1

**Life will be perfect, for heaven's the place
We'll see God, the Father and Son, face-to-face.**

Nothing evil will be allowed to enter. REVELATION 21:27

Now we see things imperfectly as in a poor mirror, but then we will see everything with perfect clarity. 1 CORINTHIANS 13:12

The throne of God and of the Lamb will be there, and his servants will worship him. And they will see his face. REVELATION 22:3-4

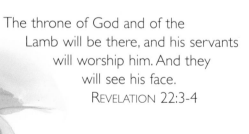

For God will be there, everywhere that you are;
And Jesus will shine like a bright morning star.

I am the bright morning star. REVELATION 22:16

**Heaven is wonderful, don't you agree?
It's simply the best place we ever could be!**

Don't be troubled. You trust God, now trust in me.
JOHN 14:1

The joys to come will last forever. 2 CORINTHIANS 4:18

The old world and its evils are gone forever.
REVELATION 21:4

About the Author

Kathleen Long Bostrom loves books—reading them and writing them!

This is Kathy's third *Little Blessings* book. The poetic questions in all three books are based on actual questions from "little hearts" in Kathy's congregation, as well as from her own family. Additional writing credits include another book of verse, titled *The World That God Made*, numerous newspaper and magazine articles, and several prizewinning sermons.

Kathy has a master of arts degree in Christian education and a master of divinity degree from Princeton Theological Seminary. She also has a bachelor of arts degree in psychology from California State University, Long Beach, California.

Wildwood, Illinois, is where Kathy lives with husband, Greg, and children Christopher, Amy, and David. She and her husband copastor the Wildwood Presbyterian Church.

Kathy hopes that her books will be used not only by parents and children but in Sunday school classes, at preschools, and in church worship settings.

About the Illustrator

Elena Kucharik, well-known Care Bears artist, has now created the *Little Blessings* characters. They appear in a line of *Little Blessings* books for young children and their families.

Born in Cleveland, Ohio, Elena received a bachelor of fine arts degree in commercial art at Kent State University. After graduation she worked as a greeting-card artist and art director at American Greetings Corporation in Cleveland.

For the past twenty-five years Elena has been a freelance illustrator. During that time she was the lead artist and developer of Care Bears, as well as a designer and illustrator for major corporations and publishers. For the past eight years Elena has been focusing her talents on illustrations for children's books.

Elena and her husband live in New Canaan, Connecticut, and have two grown daughters.

Books in the *Little Blessings* line